SUPER
BIKES

Series creator:

David Salariya was
born in Dundee, Scotland, where he studied illustration and printmaking. He has illustrated a wide range of books and has created many new series of books for publishers in the UK and overseas. In 1989 he established The Salariya Book Company. He lives in Brighton with his wife, the illustrator Shirley Willis, and their son.

Author:

Ian Graham was born
in Belfast in 1953. He studied applied physics at The City University, London, and took a postgraduate diploma in journalism at the same university, specialising in science and technology journalism. After four years as an editor of consumer electronics magazines, he became a freelance author and journalist. Since then, he has written more than one hundred children's non-fiction books and numerous magazine articles.

Artist:

Nick Hewetson was
educated in Sussex at Brighton Technical School and studied illustration at Eastbourne College of Art. He has since illustrated a wide variety of children's books.

Editor:

Karen Barker Smith

Editorial Assistant:

Stephanie Cole

Created, designed and produced by
THE SALARIYA BOOK COMPANY LTD
25 Marlborough Place, Brighton BN1 1UB

Published in Great Britain in 2001 by
Hodder Wayland, an imprint of
Hodder Children's Books

A Catalogue record for this book is available from the British Library.

ISBN 0 7502 3627 2

Printed and bound in China

Hodder Children's Books
A division of Hodder Headline Ltd
338 Euston Road, London NW1 3BH

SUPER BIKES

Written by
IAN GRAHAM

Illustrated by
NICK HEWETSON

Created and designed by
DAVID SALARIYA

W

HODDER
Wayland

An imprint of Hodder Children's Books

Contents

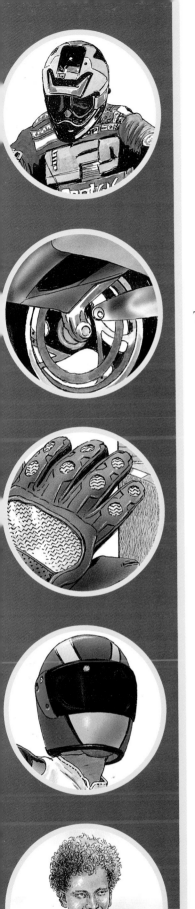

The First Motorcycles

The first motorised bicycle (right) was built by the French Michaux brothers in 1869. They fitted a steam engine to a bicycle frame.

In the 1880s and 1890s in Philadelphia, USA, the Copeland brothers built steam-powered bicycles and tricycles (below). Bicycles were less popular than tricycles because the heavy steam engine made them difficult to balance.

The first bicycles powered by engines were built in the middle of the 19th century. Only steam engines could be used at that time, and they were far from ideal. Their fuel (coal or wood) was heavy and bulky and had to be burned for some time before the engine produced enough steam to move the vehicle. The engine was noisy and the burning fuel produced thick black smoke. Occasionally, steam engine boilers exploded! Petrol engines, developed in the 1880s, were a great improvement. The moment the engine started it could move the vehicle. The first motorcycles built for sale to the public, in the early 1900s, were pedal-powered bicycles with small engines added to them. By 1914, purpose-built motorcycles were being manufactured.

In the 1880s, the German engineers Gottlieb Daimler (below) and Wilhelm Maybach developed a small, high-speed internal combustion engine suitable for powering vehicles. Instead of producing steam from water, it burned petrol. In 1885, they fitted the new engine to a wooden bicycle frame with stabiliser wheels at the sides. The engine turned the machine's rear wheel by means of a belt. The bike could manage a top speed of 19 kph. Daimler went on to build cars, but he is still remembered as the inventor of the petrol-engine motorcycle (right).

Daimler motorcycle

The German company NSU made knitting machines first and then bicycles. In 1901, it made its first motorcycle (left) by fitting a bicycle with a Swiss Zedel engine. The 234cc, 1.5 horsepower engine gave the bicycle a top speed of nearly 50 kph.

In the USA, two bicycle racers, George Hendee and Oscar Hedstrom, started making motorcycles under the name 'Indian'. Their first model was the 1904 Indian Single (below). The single cylinder engine formed part of the down-tube under the saddle. Indian motorcycles quickly became very popular because of their good design and high-quality manufacturing.

901 NSU

Cylinder

Exhaust pipe

Battery

Indian Single

INDIAN

The Suzuki company made silk-weaving looms in Japan from 1909. When the loom business slumped in the 1940s, they turned to building motorcycles instead. Their first model was the Power Free (below). The tiny 36cc engine was clipped to a standard bicycle frame.

Suzuki Power Free

Belt

Stabiliser wheels

7

Grand Prix

The first Grand Prix race was a horse race that took place in France in 1863. As motorsport grew in popularity in the early 1900s, it used the same name, Grand Prix, for its most important races. Grand Prix motorcycle races are part of an international championship. The most sought-after title in motorcycle sport is the 500cc Grand Prix world championship. There are Grand Prix classes for smaller 125cc and 250cc motorcycles. British motorcycles were the most successful in Grand Prix racing until the 1950s. Then Italian machines dominated the sport until the 1970s, when Japanese motorcycles took the lead.

John Surtees (left) set an amazing record in motorsport. He was one of the most successful motorcyclists of the late 1950s. After winning four 500cc and three 350cc world championships, he switched to car racing and reached the top in that sport as well, winning the 1964 Formula 1 championship. He later set up his own Formula 1 racing team. He is shown here sitting astride his 1956 MV Agusta Four. Its four-cylinder, 500cc engine gave it a top speed of 250 kph.

A 1960s Grand Prix race

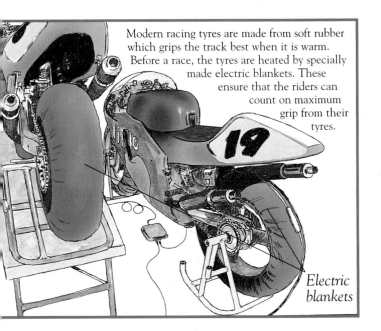

Modern racing tyres are made from soft rubber which grips the track best when it is warm. Before a race, the tyres are heated by specially made electric blankets. These ensure that the riders can count on maximum grip from their tyres.

Electric blankets

1970s

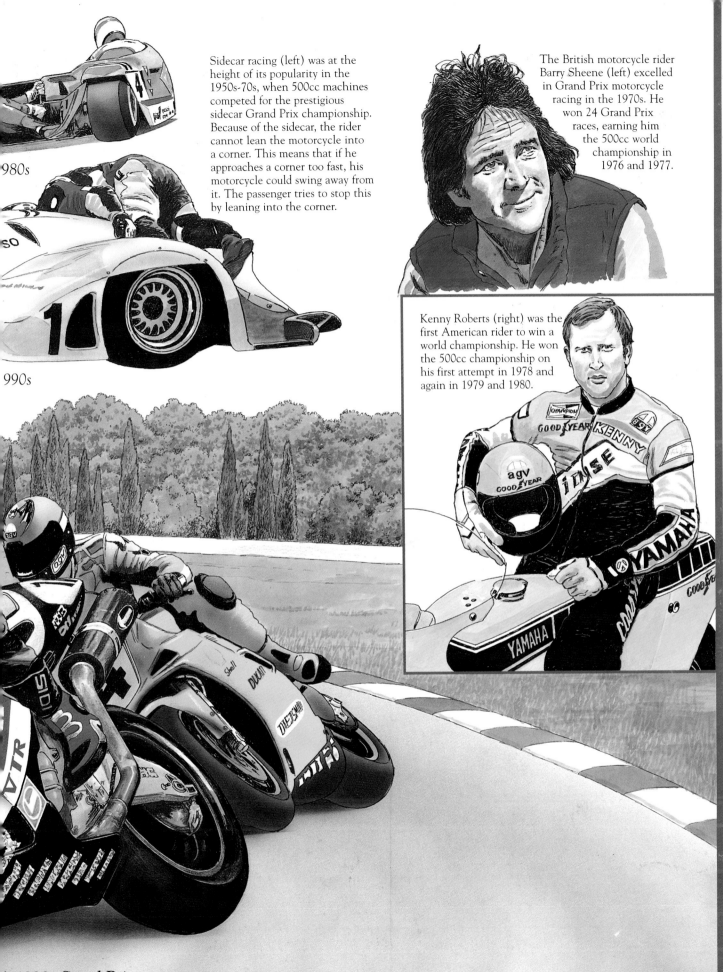

Sidecar racing (left) was at the height of its popularity in the 1950s-70s, when 500cc machines competed for the prestigious sidecar Grand Prix championship. Because of the sidecar, the rider cannot lean the motorcycle into a corner. This means that if he approaches a corner too fast, his motorcycle could swing away from it. The passenger tries to stop this by leaning into the corner.

The British motorcycle rider Barry Sheene (left) excelled in Grand Prix motorcycle racing in the 1970s. He won 24 Grand Prix races, earning him the 500cc world championship in 1976 and 1977.

Kenny Roberts (right) was the first American rider to win a world championship. He won the 500cc championship on his first attempt in 1978 and again in 1979 and 1980.

980s

990s

A 1990s Grand Prix race

Stunt Riders

Some people are not content to ride motorcycles in the normal way! Stunt riders use them to jump over things. Display teams pile people on top of them or ride them through fire. Motorcycle skiers hold onto the back of their bikes and slide along the ground behind them. Drag riders use specially designed motorcycles in one of the sport's fastest competition events. These stunts and extreme sports are highly dangerous. The teams of professionals who prepare the events and take part in them try to plan for every possibility, to make sure that everything works properly and that the riders go home in one piece. However, accidents do happen. The British stunt rider Eddie Kydd was very seriously injured when his motorcycle fell from an elevated landing ramp, ending his career. And the American stunt riders, Evel and Robbie Knievel, have both been injured while performing stunts.

Evel Knievel's son, Robbie (above), carried on in his father's footsteps as a sensational motorcycle stunt rider. His most spectacular feat was a jump over the Grand Canyon in 1999. His motorcycle soared off the take-off ramp, sailed a record-breaking distance of 70 m through the air and landed halfway down the landing ramp on the other side of the canyon. When the bike hit the rough desert floor, Knievel lost control and crashed, suffering two broken ribs and a sprained ankle.

Evel Knievel (above) is the world's best-known motorcycle stunt rider. His most famous jumps include a leap over 50 cars in the Los Angeles Coliseum. In 1974, he tried and failed to jump the Snake River Canyon in Idaho, USA, using a rocket-powered Harley-Davidson 'skycycle'. A parachute had accidentally popped out on take-off, but this meant that he floated safely to the ground. His many crash-landings are said to have broken nearly every bone in his body!

A motorcycle stunt rider soars
off the take-off ramp in a
spectacular jump (left).

Two drag riders prepare to accelerate like rockets down the straight drag strip. Small wheels at the rear of the bikes stop them from rearing up as the engines roar into life.

ntil the 1960s, organisations
at used motorcycles, such as
lice forces, often had their
n display teams that toured
e country. Outdoor events
quently featured displays by
ese teams. The riders criss-
ossed an arena in a complex
splay of precision-riding
ills. The stunts they
rformed for the crowds
cluded carrying a pyramid of
ople along on top of a line
motorcycles (left) and
mping motorcycles over
stacles, through hoops and
rough fire (right).

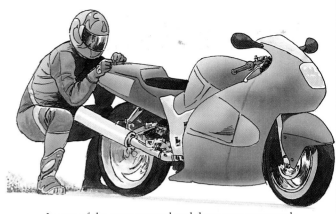

In one of the most unusual and dangerous motorcycle stunts, motorcycle skiing (above), a bike accelerates to top speed, then the rider slips backwards over the seat and steps onto the track! With showers of sparks flying from his steel-soled boots, he holds onto the back of his bike. In 1999, the record was set at an incredible speed of 251 kph by British rider Gary Rothwell, using a Suzuki Hayabusa.

Angelle Seeling (right) is one of only a handful of women to compete in motorcycle drag racing. The former intensive care nurse from Louisiana, USA, began racing drag bikes in 1996.

Motorcycle racers often celebrate winning by doing a wheelie (above). In 1999, the world record for the fastest wheelie was set at 307 kph by Swedish rider Patrik Furstenhoff on a Honda Blackbird.

15

The Yamaha YZF-R1 out-performs most comparable sports motorcycles. The key to its sizzling performance on the road is its engine power and light weight. The YZF-R1's designers looked at every part of the motorcycle and investigated ways to make it lighter. As a result of their work, the whole machine weighs only 177 kg.

The YZF-R1's silencer, fitted to the engine exhaust pipe to reduce engine noise, is made from titanium, a lightweight and corrosion-resistant metal. Its handlebars are bonded (glued) in place instead of welded, to save weight. By using a new type of plastic, the bodywork was made 25% thinner and therefore lighter than normal motorbikes. The metal wheels have thinner walls than usual and they have only three spokes. The brake discs on the front and rear wheels have been slimmed down by half a millimetre to save a few more grams. Even the instruments the rider looks at have been made lighter. The bike's four-cylinder engine is also smaller and lighter than most comparable engines. It weighs only 65 kg, but it achieves 150 bhp (brake horse-power) – that's more powerful than some small European cars up to seven times the weight of the YZF-R1. It can achieve a top speed of 280 kph.

Ducati 996

Fuel tank

Engine

Silencer

Rear view of the Yamaha YZF-R1

Brake disc

Front view of the Yamaha YZF-R1

Yamaha YZF-R1

The Italian motorcycle manufacturer Ducati is famous for its racing motorcycles. Ducatis, in the capable hands of British rider Carl Fogarty, have won four Superbike world championships. Ducati also makes highly desirable road machines such as the 996 (left). Its 996cc engine, lightweight tubular frame and streamlined shape give it a top speed of 260 kph.

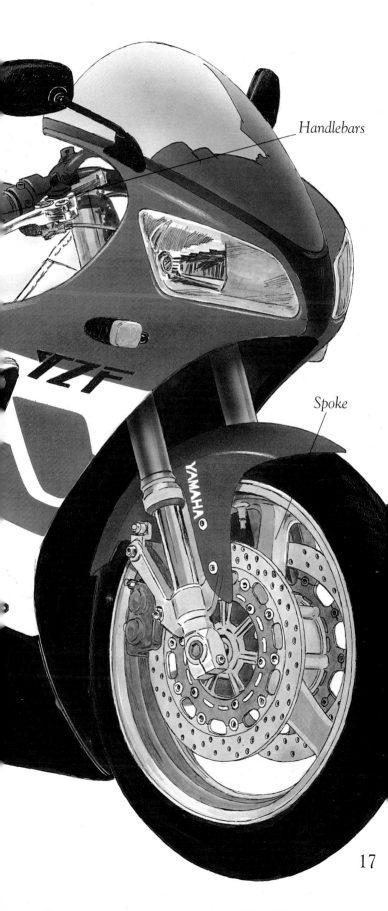

Handlebars

Spoke

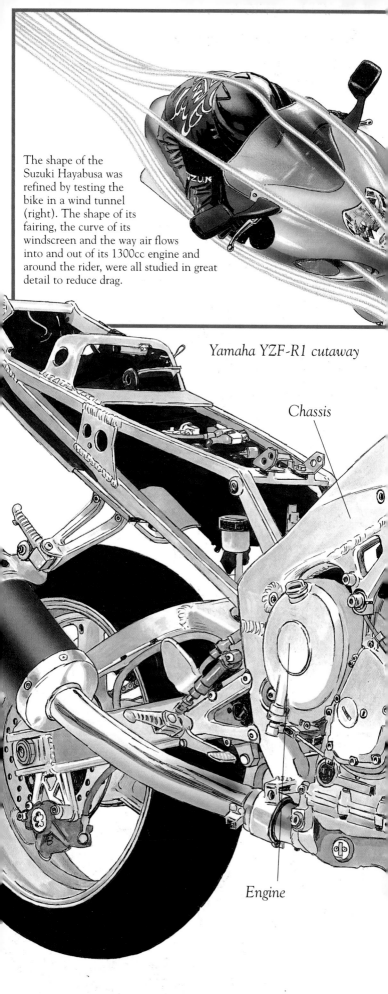

The shape of the Suzuki Hayabusa was refined by testing the bike in a wind tunnel (right). The shape of its fairing, the curve of its windscreen and the way air flows into and out of its 1300cc engine and around the rider, were all studied in great detail to reduce drag.

Yamaha YZF-R1 cutaway

Chassis

Engine

Suzuki Hayabusa

The Suzuki Hayabusa (above) is the world's fastest production motorcycle. It can reach an amazing top speed of 300 kph. It was named Hayabusa after a Japanese falcon that can also cut through the air at this speed.

Radiator

High Performance

High performance sports road bikes are built to look like racing machines. Their sporty performance is produced by a combination of engine power, a smooth shape and light weight. Small sports motorcycles have engines with two cylinders, while the biggest machines have four-cylinder engines. If two cylinders are set at an angle to each other, forming a V shape, the engine is called a V-twin. A smooth cover called a fairing hides most of the engine and makes the bike more streamlined. The heavier any vehicle is, the more engine power it needs. Every gram saved improves a motorcycle's performance, so sports-bike designers put a great deal of effort into saving weight wherever possible.

Suzuki TL1000R

The Suzuki TL1000R (above) is a sleek, streamlined machine. Its big 1,000cc V-twin engine gives it a top speed of more than 240 kph.

Honda's Fireblade (below) is a super all-round sports bike with a winning blend of power, speed and balance. Its 900cc four-cylinder engine gives a top speed of 265 kph.

Honda Fireblade

19

Cal Rayborn (below) won the Daytona 200 race in Florida, USA, in 1968 and 1969. In 1970 he set a motorcycle land speed record of 427 kph. His sparkling career was cut short when he died while racing in New Zealand in 1973.

Cal Rayborn

In endurance races motorcycles have to visit the pits from time to time to be re-fuelled and have their tyres changed (below). During these pit-stops, which usually take only a few seconds, riders often change over too. Fast pit-stops are essential because a race lasting several hours can be won or lost by just a fraction of a second.

Super Stars

Motorcycle sports test riders and their machines in many different ways. Long-distance endurance races last for up to 24 hours. The most famous include the 24-hour Le Mans race in France and the Suzuka eight-hour race in Japan. Teams of two or three riders take turns to keep each motorcycle on the track for the whole race without a break. Road races, such as the Tourist Trophy races held on the Isle of Man, challenge riders to compete at high speeds on normal roads with bumps, bends, kerbs and roadside signs. One form of motorcycle sport, superbike racing, has become hugely popular in recent years. It began in the USA in the 1970s, using modified road bikes. Some of the most successful Grand Prix motorcyclists started racing on superbikes.

Carl Fogarty (left) is one of the most successful riders in motorcycle sport but he has never competed in Grand Prix races. He is a champion superbike rider. Superbike riders compete on motorcycles that are very similar to road bikes. Few modifications to the bikes are allowed, so the races are close-fought. Nowadays, superbike racing rivals Grand Prix racing for popularity and excitement.

Refuelling

Superbike rider

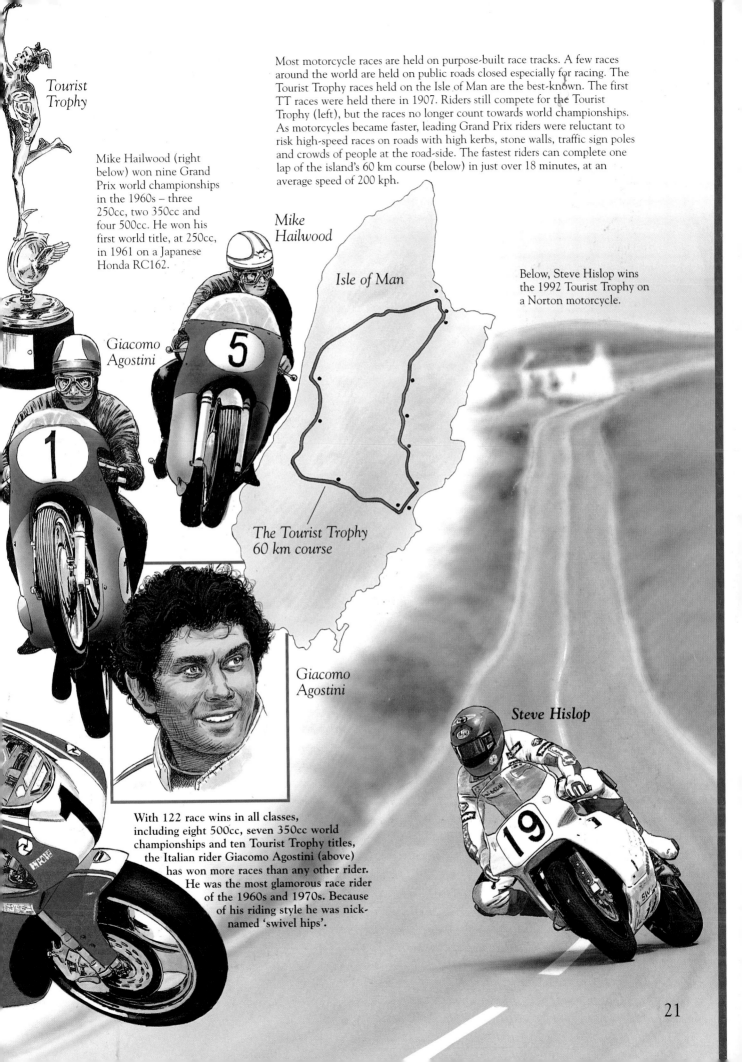

Tourist Trophy

Mike Hailwood (right below) won nine Grand Prix world championships in the 1960s – three 250cc, two 350cc and four 500cc. He won his first world title, at 250cc, in 1961 on a Japanese Honda RC162.

Mike Hailwood

Giacomo Agostini

Most motorcycle races are held on purpose-built race tracks. A few races around the world are held on public roads closed especially for racing. The Tourist Trophy races held on the Isle of Man are the best-known. The first TT races were held there in 1907. Riders still compete for the Tourist Trophy (left), but the races no longer count towards world championships. As motorcycles became faster, leading Grand Prix riders were reluctant to risk high-speed races on roads with high kerbs, stone walls, traffic sign poles and crowds of people at the road-side. The fastest riders can complete one lap of the island's 60 km course (below) in just over 18 minutes, at an average speed of 200 kph.

Isle of Man

Below, Steve Hislop wins the 1992 Tourist Trophy on a Norton motorcycle.

The Tourist Trophy 60 km course

Giacomo Agostini

With 122 race wins in all classes, including eight 500cc, seven 350cc world championships and ten Tourist Trophy titles, the Italian rider Giacomo Agostini (above) has won more races than any other rider. He was the most glamorous race rider of the 1960s and 1970s. Because of his riding style he was nick- named 'swivel hips'.

Steve Hislop

21

Motocross rider

Dirt Devils

Motorcycles are raced on every type of surface. Loose surfaces like sand, dirt and shale are difficult to race on because motorcycle tyres can't grip them well. When riders lean their bikes over to go round corners, they have to put a foot down to stop the bikes from falling over. One of the most popular loose surface sports is supercross, or motocross, which involves racing round a bumpy, muddy course. Speedway events are races held on very slippery oval-shaped tracks made from dirt or shale. Races are also held on the slippiest surface of all – ice. There are even races through deserts.

Motocross bike

A motocross bike (above) has very springy wheels that can bounce up and down a long way. This helps to keep the bike level across bumpy ground. Speedway bikes (left) are light and low and they have no brakes. They burn methanol instead of petrol, which is held in a tiny 2-litre tank. Top speed is less important than fast acceleration – a speedway bike can go from a standing start to 95 kph in two seconds. Desert bikes (far left) are completely different. They are bigger and much heavier – perhaps four times the weight of a speedway bike. They are also higher off the ground to cope with rough terrain, and they have a bigger fuel tank.

Desert bike

Speedway bike

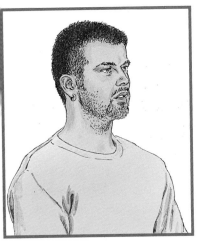

The US rider Jeremy McGrath (left) started racing bikes when he was 5 years old. Since then he has won the 1995 AMA 250cc National Motocross Championship, the 1994 and 1995 FIM World Supercross Championships and the AMA 250cc Supercross Championships in 1993, 1994, 1995, 1996, 1998 and 1999.

Desert racing

The world's most famous desert race is the Paris-Dakar rally, in which riders cross the Sahara Desert in North Africa. It can be difficult to find the right route in the desert and getting lost is dangerous. In long desert races, groups of riders often stay within sight of each other for safety.

Motorcycle trials are completely different. They involve riding over large obstacles such as rocks and tree trunks. Unlike other loose surface sports, trials riders are not allowed to put a foot down to steady themselves. Regulations control the bike design for these various events, so that they are evenly matched and the races are close and exciting.

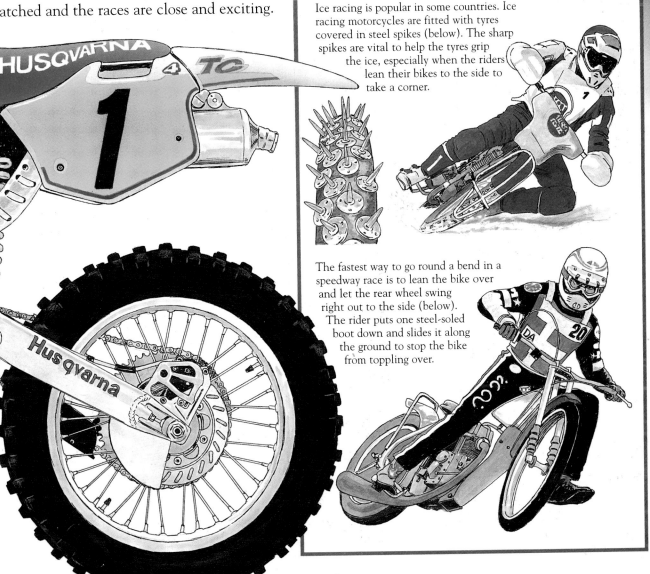

Ice racing is popular in some countries. Ice racing motorcycles are fitted with tyres covered in steel spikes (below). The sharp spikes are vital to help the tyres grip the ice, especially when the riders lean their bikes to the side to take a corner.

The fastest way to go round a bend in a speedway race is to lean the bike over and let the rear wheel swing right out to the side (below). The rider puts one steel-soled boot down and slides it along the ground to stop the bike from toppling over.

Honda X-Wing

Some future motorcycles will combine the advanced engineering and design of today's motorcycles with the safety and comfort of today's scooters. The 1500cc Honda X-Wing (above) is a prototype of one of these future 'super-scooters'.

Some designers have produced very dramatic versions of what they think future motorcycles might look like. This stunning dream bike (right) is based on a real motorcycle, the 1000cc Suzuki TL1000S sports road bike.

Bikes to Come

Motorcycle design is always developing. By using metals such as aluminium and new materials such as carbon fibre, bikes can be made to weigh less, which means they use less power. Because of this they burn less fuel, which is kinder to the environment. More efficient engines further reduce the amount of fuel burned. The shape of a motorcycle must be practical – there has to be enough space for the engine, fuel tank and other parts. Faster sports bikes have a streamlined fairing to cut air resistance. However, motorcycles are not just practical vehicles. Their appearance changes with changing fashions, new ideas from designers, the popularity of certain motorcycle sports and even the types of motorcycles that appear in films.

futuristic bike design based the Suzuki TL1000S

Aprilia's Moto 6.5 roadster (below) looks very different from its usual style of road-going models. The Italian manufacturer Aprilia is well-known for its racing motorcycles and road-going sports motorcycles. Technical advances and engineering developments on the race track are used to improve the design and performance of its road bikes. The Moto 6.5 roadster was created for Aprilia by the French designer Philippe Starck. His aim was to combine the most advanced technology with a timeless look that would not date.

Aprilia Moto 6.5

Harley-Davidson

Harley-Davidson

Motorcycles have grown bigger over the years but they will never equal the biggest Harley-Davidson in the world (above). It was built by the owner of a motorcycle shop in California, USA. The 'rider' sits inside the five-tonne machine which is 14 m long and stands 8 m high. Its five-litre Cadillac car engine gives it a top speed of 130 kph.

The latest motorcycles are not always sleek and streamlined machines. New bikes that look as if they were made long ago are popular too (left). This is called 'retro styling'. In the future, some motorcycles may copy the designs of today's machines.

Bikes Safety

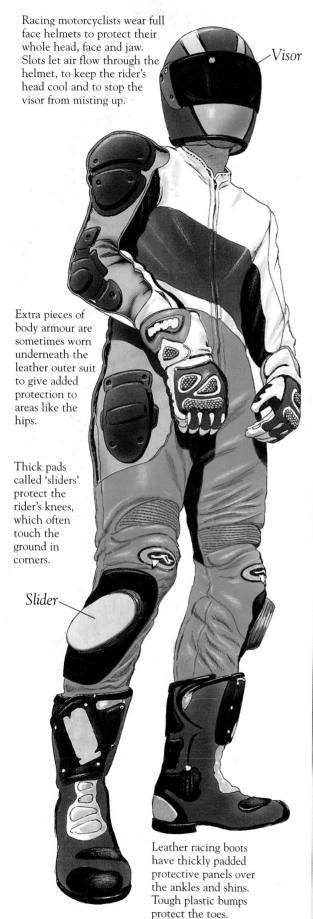

Racing clothing

Racing motorcyclists wear full face helmets to protect their whole head, face and jaw. Slots let air flow through the helmet, to keep the rider's head cool and to stop the visor from misting up.

Visor

Extra pieces of body armour are sometimes worn underneath the leather outer suit to give added protection to areas like the hips.

Thick pads called 'sliders' protect the rider's knees, which often touch the ground in corners.

Slider

Leather racing boots have thickly padded protective panels over the ankles and shins. Tough plastic bumps protect the toes.

It is vital that motorcyclists protect themselves from injury by wearing the right clothing. Head protection is especially important. A motorcycle helmet works in two ways to prevent brain damage. Its hard outer shell stops the skull from being fractured or crushed, while its soft lining cushions the brain. Clothing protects the rest of the body from scrapes and cuts. The clothing is thicker and tougher over easily damaged areas of the body like the knees, elbows and the backs of the hands. Leather is a favourite material for motorcycle clothing because it wears away when scraped along the ground without tearing. Tough plastic spine protectors are sometimes worn inside the clothes to give added back protection.

Racing motorcyclists take their machines to the limit (right). A momentary loss of tyre grip can upset the delicate balance of the bike, especially when cornering. It can make a bike slide out of a corner and spill the rider onto the track. Racing motorcyclists wear all-in-one suits called leathers. Leathers give a rider's body a smooth outline to cut drag and to provide some skin protection if the rider comes off the bike and slides along the track. Even so, riders can suffer burns from friction between the track and their leathers.

Reinforced
gloves

Full face helmet

Leathers

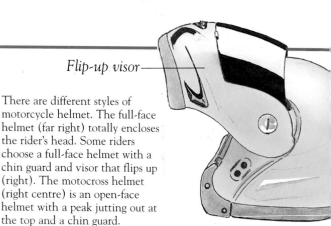

Flip-up visor

There are different styles of motorcycle helmet. The full-face helmet (far right) totally encloses the rider's head. Some riders choose a full-face helmet with a chin guard and visor that flips up (right). The motocross helmet (right centre) is an open-face helmet with a peak jutting out at the top and a chin guard.

The latest motorcycle gloves (right) are made from leather with the knuckles and wrist strengthened with a carbon-fibre material called Kevlar. The gloves are tightened onto the hand with Velcro straps so that they will not come off in an accident.

Safety clothing for motorcyclists is as important on public roads as on racetracks. One-piece leather racing suits are worn by some sports-bike riders but most motorcyclists wear jackets and trousers. These are often made from leather but they are also now made from a range of man-made materials, which are lightweight, waterproof and tough. The jackets and trousers often have linings that can be taken out in warm weather.

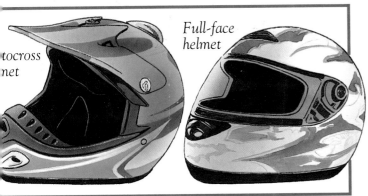

tocross
net

Full-face
helmet

Full-face helmet

Tear-resistant
jacket

Leather
gloves

Armoured
jeans

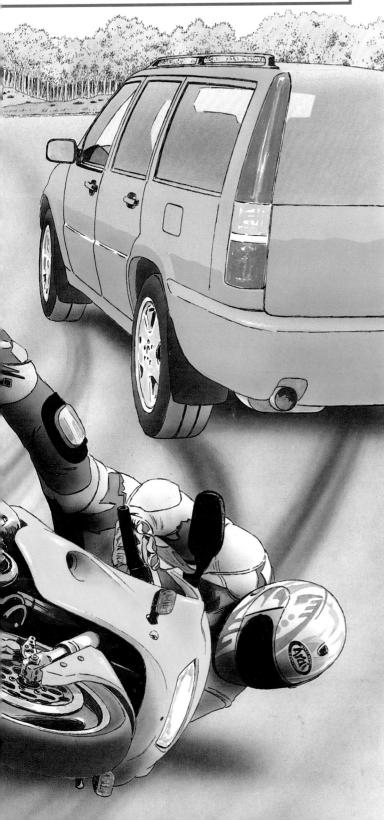

Motorcycle boots are
made in different styles.
Many riders like the
classic black leather boot,
while others prefer the
more casual desert boot.
They support the toes
and ankles. Some protect
the shins too.

Some motorcycle safety
clothing is made to look
more like normal casual
clothes. Armoured jeans,
for example, have tough
pads sewn into the
material to protect the
rider in case of an
accident.

29

Glossary

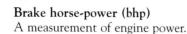

Aluminium
A light, silver-coloured metal.

Brake horse-power (bhp)
A measurement of engine power.

Carbon fibre
A solid, strong and light material that can withstand high temperatures. It is used to make motorcyclists' safety clothing.

cc
Cubic centimetres; these are the units used to measure the size of the cylinders in an engine.

Combustion
Another word for burning.

Cylinder
One of the tube-shaped chambers in an engine where fuel is burned.

Disc brakes
Brakes that work by using pads to grip a steel disc fixed to the wheel.

Drag
Air resistance, a force that slows down a motorcycle, caused by air pushing against it.

Dragster
An immensely powerful motorcycle used for drag racing.

Fairing
A streamlined covering that wraps around the engine of a motorcycle to make the bike slip through the air more easily.

Fuel
A liquid such as petrol that is changed to a vapour and burned inside an engine.

Horsepower
A measure of how fast an engine converts the energy in its fuel into movement energy.

Internal combustion engine
A type of engine which burns fuel inside the engine.

Kevlar
A tough man-made material used in clothing for motorcyclists. It is five times stronger than the same weight of steel.

Pits
Garages at the side of racetracks where bikes can be re-fuelled and riders changed.

Prototype
A model of a bike, used to test the design before the bike goes into production.

Scooter
A light motorcycle with a footboard for resting the feet on between the engine and front wheel.

Shale
A surface of fine, gravelly rock.

Silencer
A pipe-shaped chamber attached to a motorcycle engine's exhaust pipe to reduce engine noise.

Titanium
An extremely tough yet lightweight metal that does not corrode and can withstand very high temperatures.

Tubular frame
A motorcycle frame made from metal tubes welded together.

V-twin engine
A type of motorcycle engine with 2 cylinders set at an angle to each other, forming the shape of the letter 'V'.

Welded
Pieces of metal joined together by heating.

Super Bike Facts

The badge of the Japanese motorcycle manufacturer, Yamaha, shows three tuning forks because the company originally made musical instruments.

Racing bikes use tyres without any tread, called slicks. They can only be used on a dry track. In wet weather, tyres with tread, called wets, are used.

The lap record at the Isle of Man TT race is held by Superbike champion Carl Fogarty. In 1992, he set the fastest ever average lap speed of 197 kph.

John Surtees is the only person to win Grand Prix championships on both two and four wheels.

Not all motorcycles have two wheels! Four-wheeled motorcycles called quad bikes are used for sport, recreation and farming. Farmers use them to get around land more quickly than on foot and to help round up animals.

On a fast lap, the rear tyre of a racing bike gets hotter than boiling water. Temperatures around 125°C are common.

Since the beginning of the motorcycle industry more than 2,000 different makes of motorbike have been produced.

The first purpose-built motor race track in the world was laid at Brooklands in Surrey. It was closed in 1938.

In 1923 the American E.J. Christie designed a large single-wheeled motorbike, which he claimed would reach a speed of 400 kph. However, there is no evidence that his machine was a success.

Chronology

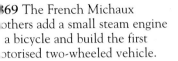

869 The French Michaux
others add a small steam engine
a bicycle and build the first
otorised two-wheeled vehicle.

885 Gottlieb Daimler and
ilhelm Maybach build the
st petrol engine motorcycle.

888 John Boyd Dunlop invents
e pneumatic (air-filled) tyre.

894 The first mass-produced
otorcycle is manufactured
Heinrich Hildebrand and
lois Wolfmüller.

899 The first military
otorcycle is built for service in
e Boer War. A Maxim machine-
n is fitted to a French de Dion
otorised tricycle.

902 The first motor scooter is
ilt in France. It is called an
utofauteuil, which means
otor-armchair!

904 The first Harley-Davidson
otorcycle, called the Silent Gray
ellow, is manufactured in the
nited States.

906 Motorcycle racing begins on
e Isle of Man.

907 The first Tourist Trophy
otorcycle race is held on the
le of Man.

909 The first motorcycle speed
cord, 122 kph, is set by William
ook at the Brooklands race track
England.

910 The sidecar is invented.

911 The 'Mountain Course' is
sed for the first time for the Isle
Man Tourist Trophy motorcycle
ice. It is still used today.

912 Carl Stevens Clancy
ecomes the first person to ride a
otorcycle around the world.

913 The first motorcycle with
n electric starter motor, the
dian Hendee Special, is

manufactured, but electric starter
motors do not become
commonplace until the 1960s.

1914 Motorcycles are fitted with
machine guns for use in World
War I. Other motorcycles are
fitted with sidecars and used
as ambulances.

1915 The American company
Indian becomes the biggest
motorcycle manufacturer in
the world.

1920 The first official motorcycle
land speed record, 167 kph, is
set by Ernie Walker on an Indian
motorcycle at Daytona Beach,
USA.

1937 A Harley-Davidson model
61 ridden by Joe Petrali sets an
ocean-level land speed record for
motorcycles of 219 kph.

1939 The first motorcycles
designed specifically as military
motorcycles are built for use in
World War II.

1958 A standard specification for
motorcycle helmets is developed
in the USA after the death of an
amateur rider, Peter Snell, because
of poor helmet design.

1960 John Surtees wins the last of
his four 500cc and three 350cc
Grand Prix championships.

1961 Mike Hailwood wins the
250cc Grand Prix championship,
the first of three 250cc, two 350cc
and four 500cc world titles.

1966 Bob Leppan sets a new
motorcycle land speed record
of 395 kph.

1970 US motorcyclist Cal
Rayborn sets a new motorcycle
land speed record of 427 kph.

1973 Cal Rayborn is killed while
racing in New Zealand.

1974 US stunt rider Evel
Knievel's attempt to jump his

rocket-powered motorcycle over
the Snake River Canyon in Idaho,
USA, fails when a parachute
opens too early.

1975 Italian motorcycle racer
Giacomo Agostini wins the 500cc
Grand Prix championship, the last
of his eight 500cc and seven
350cc titles.

1978 Donald Vesco sets a
motorcycle land speed record of
512 kph on his *Lightning Bolt*
motorcycle, a specially built
machine powered by two
Kawasaki motorcycle engines.

1979 The first Paris-Dakar rally
is held.

1980 Kenny Roberts wins the last
of his three consecutive 500cc
Grand Prix championships.

1981 US stunt rider Evel Knievel
retires.

1983 The first rocket-propelled
motorcycle is built by Dutch drag
racer Henk Vink. It can reach a
top speed of 400 kph.

1989 The first World Superbike
Championship is held. It is won
by Fred Merkel on a Honda.

1990 Dave Campos, riding a
Harley-Davidson powered
machine, sets a new motorcycle
land speed record of 518 kph.

1994 Mike Doohan wins the first
of his five 500cc Grand Prix
championships.

1999 US stunt rider Robbie
Knievel jumps his motorcycle
over the Grand Canyon in
Colorado, USA.

2000 Robbie Knievel jumps
his motorcycle over a moving
railway locomotive.

Index